THE ADVENTURE OF LIFE

Jean-Benoît Durand

Illustrations by Robin Gindre

GECKO PRESS

English edition first published in 2010 by Gecko Press
PO Box 9335, Marion Square, Wellington 6141, New Zealand
Email: info@geckopress.com

National Library of New Zealand Cataloguing-in-Publication Data

Durand, Jean-Benoît.
Vie à petits pas.
The adventure of life / by Jean- Benoît Durand ; illustrated by Robin Gindre.
ISBN 978-1-877467-50-9
(Step by step)
1. Biology—Juvenile literature. 2. Earth sciences—Juvenile
 literature. [1. Biology. 2. Earth sciences.] I. Gindre, Robin.
II. Title. III. Series: Step by step (Gecko Press)
500—dc 22

Translated by Jean Anderson
Edited by Raymond Huber
Typeset by Archetype, New Zealand
Printed by Everbest, China

For more curiously good books, please visit www.geckopress.com

Contents

I

A PLANET FOR LIFE

The universe is born

As far as we know, Earth is the only planet in the solar system where life exists. It's home to at least 1.7 million different species of plants and animals, including nearly seven billion humans. But before people appeared on the scene, what was here? There was once a time when Earth did not exist ...

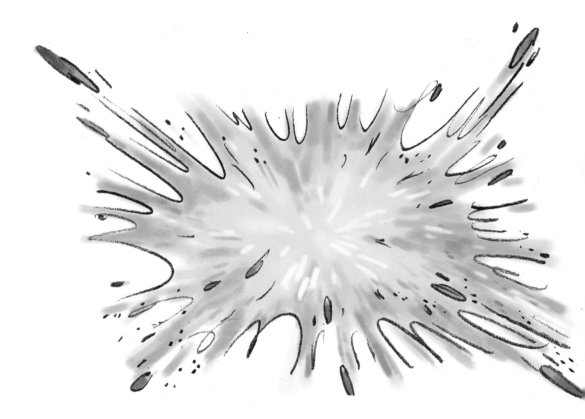

The origins of the universe

Most scientists agree the universe was formed almost 13.7 billion years ago by a massive explosion they call the 'Big Bang'. A source of very hot energy suddenly exploded. In a fraction of a second, an enormous amount of matter burst free and expanded, like a balloon stretching. This matter was like a lumpy soup made from nature's basic ingredients. As the universe expanded and cooled, particles clumped together to create atoms, stars and galaxies. Earth is part of the Milky Way galaxy.

The origins of our solar system

Our solar system began as an immense cloud of gas and dust swirling in space 4.7 billion years ago. As it contracted, the centre of this cloud became a star which we now call our Sun.

The dust formed into rocky clumps which became bigger and bigger as they circled the Sun.

Over millions of years, these masses turned into thousands of little planets. They kept crashing into each other until there were only a few left. This is how the planets of our solar system were created. One of them is Earth.

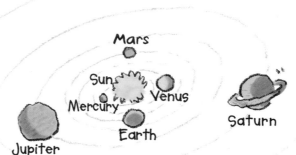

Uranus

Mars

Sun

Mercury

Venus

Earth

Saturn

Jupiter

Neptune

Pluto (although scientists now say this isn't a true planet)

A fiery birth

When Earth first appeared 4.6 billion years ago, it looked nothing like the planet you know. You wouldn't have been able to live there. Just imagine: meteorite showers; volcanoes everywhere; hot as an oven; and the air filled with toxic gases.

After a few million years, Earth finally settled down.

The atmosphere filled with water vapour which caused heavy rainfall. There was so much rain that the planet cooled, hardened and was covered by oceans.

An environment to support life

Earth is the only planet in the solar system that has liquid water. And since every living thing needs water to survive, ours is the only known planet where life can exist. Plants, animals and humans are mostly made of water.

Your body is about 65% water!

Without the Sun and the atmosphere, there wouldn't be any living things. The Sun gives us the light and warmth we need to grow. The atmosphere around Earth contains oxygen which allows us to breathe. It also protects us from being burned by the Sun's rays.

Are we alone in the universe?

As far as we know, Earth is the only planet that is home to people, animals and plants. There are many other planets in the universe and it's possible that the conditions needed for life may exist somewhere else (although it may not be life as we know it). These other planets are too far away for us to visit any time soon. Meanwhile, scientists are observing and listening to the universe and watching for light signals. There's nothing to report so far!

Hey, I was only joking!

The seeds of life

There were no living creatures when Earth was first formed. So how did life begin? Many scientists think that life was born in a 'primeval soup' about 3.7 billion years ago. The soup was produced by a mixture of gas and water, and was heated by volcanoes.

The first life forms were microscopic, single-celled organisms. These bacteria are almost identical to the ones we have today.

All the organisms now living on Earth are descended from these first cells. Most plants and animals are made up of several billion cells. Humans are the outright cell champions, though, with around 100,000 billion of them. Our cells are specialised: some are for breathing, some for digestion, others for the nervous system.

Cells

What do a man, a mouse and a tree have in common? It's hard to think of anything. But if you examine these living things under a microscope, you'll see that all three are made up of cells. So why don't they look alike?

The answer is that there are many different types of cells. The shape and size of cells vary depending on their type. But all cells are built to the same pattern, and each of them is a bit like a very busy little factory.

Inside an animal cell

The control centre is the **nucleus**. It contains the genetic information, ▶ in the form of DNA.

The **mitochondria** provide the energy, like a motor.

The **membrane** that surrounds the cell is like the factory's security guard, screening everything that passes through.

The **cytoplasm** that fills the cell looks like a jelly. ◀ Inside it are the workers responsible for keeping the machine running.

Cell suicide

Most of our cells are programmed to renew themselves regularly. For example, the cells of our skin die, fall off and are replaced by new ones. This sort of cell 'suicide' is also how trees get rid of their leaves in the autumn.

11

The first living creatures

About a billion years ago, cells grouped together to create the first multi-celled life forms. These little creatures were still very simple. They looked like tiny jellyfish and floated wherever the ocean currents took them.

The first real animals appeared on Earth 650 million years ago. From studying fossils, we know that their bodies were soft and that they didn't have spines or skeletons.

An explosion of life

At the beginning of the Paleozoic time period, 540 million years ago, life took on a variety of forms. Thousands of different species appeared in the oceans.

Trilobites were the most common. Their bodies had three lobes ('tri' means three) and jointed legs. They were about ten centimetres long.

Hallucigenia (named because it looked really freaky) had seven pairs of legs and seven pairs of spikes. It was 2.5 centimetres long.

Ammonites were molluscs (like squid) with shells. By changing the amount of gas inside their shells, they could go up and down in the water, like tiny submarines.

The **anomalocaris** was the largest living creature of its time. It was 60 centimetres long.

Weird fish

The first fish appeared 500 million years ago. They looked nothing like fish today. Their bodies were covered in bony plates and they had no jaws. But they had a spine, which means they were the first vertebrates, before reptiles, birds and mammals. Muscles would later attach themselves to these spines, allowing fish to move around faster.

Fifty million years later, fish had changed a lot. They had jaws and teeth to defend or attack, fins for steering, and scales that helped them glide quickly through the water.

Why were the first creatures born underwater?

None of the first single-celled organisms could have developed on Earth's surface. This is because the ozone layer didn't exist yet to protect them from the Sun's deadly rays. Water acted as a shield against toxic gases and solar radiation.

Conquering dry land

Plants such as algae and ferns were first to emerge from the water, 400 million years ago. They probably moved onto the land in stages, taking advantage of low tides. Since the water and minerals that plants needed to survive were only available from the soil, they developed roots to adapt to the land environment.

About 100 million years later, plants had adapted so well to life on land that a large part of the planet was covered by giant forests. Certain trees were as tall as 30 metres, and some ferns were as big as trees.

Shortly after plants, insects ventured out onto land. The first of these were tiny invertebrates with shells, followed by many species that looked like centipedes and scorpions.

Some insects began to fly to escape from predators. Dragonflies as big as seagulls flew over the prehistoric forests.

The first land vertebrates were amphibians, the ancestors of frogs. These animals had one big advantage: they were able to breathe under water as well as on land.

The **ichthyostega** was one of the first to poke its nose out of the water. Its head, tail and long body were still those of a fish, but its seven-toed fins were almost like feet and its lungs allowed it to breathe air.

From reptiles to dinosaurs

The descendants of early amphibians adapted even better to life out of the water. These were the reptiles. Three hundred million years ago, reptiles took over Earth thanks to their amazing 'invention' — the eggshell. The most famous reptiles to evolve were the dinosaurs (meaning 'terrible lizards'), who would come to rule the planet for 155 million years. Over 800 different dinosaur species have been discovered.

An amazing invention

Amphibians were not able to go far onto land. They had to lay their eggs in water or they'd dry out. Reptiles didn't have to worry about this because their babies developed inside a protective shell. It was lined with a membrane which kept the embryo from drying out. Thanks to this natural invention, reptiles quickly spread across the whole planet, even its driest parts.

During the Mesozoic era, dinosaurs ruled the world. Some were among the biggest animals that Earth has ever seen. The **brachiosaurus** was as tall as a four-storeyed building. It weighed as much as a dozen elephants. Other dinosaurs were no bigger than chickens and spent their days grazing quietly.

Small but speedy

The first dinosaurs appeared about 250 million years ago, during the **Triassic** period. At this time, all the continents were joined in a single land mass which is known as Pangaea. The climate was warm and dry all year. Dinosaurs were not very large at first, but they did have one big advantage: their legs were positioned underneath their bodies. This allowed them to run, unlike other reptiles that crawled on the ground.

Jurassic giants

During the **Jurassic** period (200 million years ago), the planet was covered in vegetation which provided a lot of food for herbivorous animals. These vegetarians included the gigantic sauropods, such as the seismosaurus, whose necks were so long they could chew the tops of the trees.

A very mixed bunch

The seasons began in the **Cretaceous** period, 145 million years ago. Summers were warm and wet; winters were cool. This allowed the first flowering plants to develop. Dinosaurs became much more varied. Large herds of placid herbivores, such as iguanodons, were preyed on by the most terrifying predator of all – the tyrannosaurus rex.

The two main dinosaur families

Paleontologists divide dinosaurs into two main groups, depending on the shape and position of the bone at the base of their backs. Those with a lizard pelvis are called saurischians. Those with a bird pelvis are ornithischians.

Saurischians

Theropods ('animal footed') are carnivorous bipeds (two legs) with well-developed muscles.

Sauropods ('lizard footed') are large herbivorous quadrupeds (four legs) with long necks.

Ornithischians

Ornithopods ('bird footed') are herbivorous quadrupeds or bipeds.

Pachycephalosaurs ('thick-headed lizards') are herbivorous bipeds whose heads are protected by a helmet.

Ceratopsians ('horned dinosaurs') are herbivorous quadrupeds with a ruff-shaped collar and long horns on their heads.

Ankylosaurs ('armoured lizards') are herbivorous quadrupeds covered in plates of armour and spines. Their tails end in a bony sphere.

Stegosaurs ('plated lizards') are herbivorous quadrupeds with a row of triangular plates running down their backs and spikes at the end of their tails.

The mystery of extinction

No human being has ever seen a living dinosaur. Why? Because they all disappeared 65 million years ago at the end of the Cretaceous period. The first humans wouldn't appear until 63 million years later.

The most generally accepted explanation for the extinction of the dinosaurs is that a gigantic meteor fell to Earth and landed violently. The impact may have set off a tsunami and raised a cloud of dust that blocked out the Sun for months or years. Deprived of light, the plants would have died, leaving the herbivorous dinosaurs without food. Then the carnivorous dinosaurs would have no herbivores to eat, and would have died out too.

What survived?

Curiously, the catastrophe that wiped out the dinosaurs didn't affect every living creature. It's thought that three out of every ten species survived. Amongst the survivors were some reptiles, mammals, amphibians and insects.

Dinosaurs will never return to Earth, but thanks to fossils we know their descendants are still with us. For example, all of the planet's birds are descended from the archeopteryx, itself a descendant of a small carnivorous dinosaur.

The **archeopteryx** is the oldest known bird. It lived 130 million years ago, and had teeth, claws and wings. To fly, it probably had to climb into the trees before throwing itself clumsily into the air.

Studying fossils

Since the beginnings of life on Earth, many millions of species of animals and plants have existed. Most have disappeared now, but we can still see some of them as fossils. Without the magical process of fossilisation, the past would remain a mystery.

Fossilisation

Usually when an animal dies, its flesh is eaten by scavengers and its bones crumble away to dust. If it dies near a sea, lake or swamp, its body may be covered over by mud. The hardest parts, such as the teeth, bones or shell, are slowly transformed into stone.

1. A dead animal sinks to the bottom of the sea or lake.

2. The body is covered by mud or sediment. The flesh rots.

3. Over time, the chemicals in the sediment change the skeleton into stone. It becomes a fossil.

4. Millions of years later, the fossil appears as if by magic, usually because of erosion.

Living fossils

Only a few species of prehistoric animals have survived until today.

The **nautilus** is a shellfish that first appeared 360 million years ago and has barely changed since then. It lives in the Pacific and Indian Oceans.

The **coelacanth**, a fish with a bony skeleton, has been around for about 400 million years. It was first sighted in the Indian Ocean in 1938.

The **limulus** (known as the horseshoe crab) is another prehistoric survivor often spotted in the Pacific. This invertebrate has a shell like a tortoise and has been on Earth for 500 million years.

Dinosaur hunters

Since the mid-1850s, paleontologists have been searching for dinosaur fossils. When a bone or skeleton is discovered, it's gently separated from the rock with a chisel and then a small brush. Before moving it, the paleontologists make drawings and take photographs of the site to record the position of the bones. Finally, the fossil is coated in plaster to protect it while it is transported.

II

FROM EARLY MAMMALS
TO THE HUMAN RACE

Mammals multiply

Mammals appeared at almost the same time as dinosaurs, about 225 million years ago. But as long as dinosaurs walked the planet, mammals kept out of the way. They only came out at night and grew no bigger than mice.

When the dinosaurs disappeared, mammals began to dominate the planet.

At the start of the Cenozoic era (65 million years ago), thousands of different mammals quickly adapted to every possible environment. They didn't look like today's species but they hinted at the range that would develop later. There were herbivores, insectivores, carnivores, rodents … Several species lived in the sea – the grandparents of whales. Over time, some mammals became gigantic, such as the mammoths.

Babies growing inside their mothers

Like reptiles, the first mammals laid eggs. Towards the end of the Mesozoic era, 120 million years ago, most of them had a new way of making babies. The embryo now developed inside the mother's womb, which is much safer than laying eggs.

Dinner's ready!

Mammals are so named because they have mammary glands (teats). Mothers use their teats to give milk to their babies, which means babies don't have to find their own food.

Why didn't mammals disappear at the same time as the dinosaurs?

Unlike dinosaurs, mammals rarely suffer from the cold. They have little internal heaters that keep their bodies warm, even in freezing weather. This is probably why they were able to withstand the cooling climate when dinosaurs were not. Mammals were also smaller then, so they could survive on little food.

The most gifted of the mammals

Compared with other life forms that have existed for hundreds of millions of years, humans are a recent arrival on Earth. They first appeared in Africa two to three million years ago. To begin with, humans were similar to monkeys, but have been evolving ever since.

Humans are not descended from monkeys, but we do share a common ancestor. Orang-utans, gorillas and chimpanzees are our cousins! We all belong to the same family of mammals, the primates, which appeared on Earth 67 million years ago.

Primates are mammals that are able to walk on two legs. They use their hands and feet to grasp objects and their brain is well-developed.

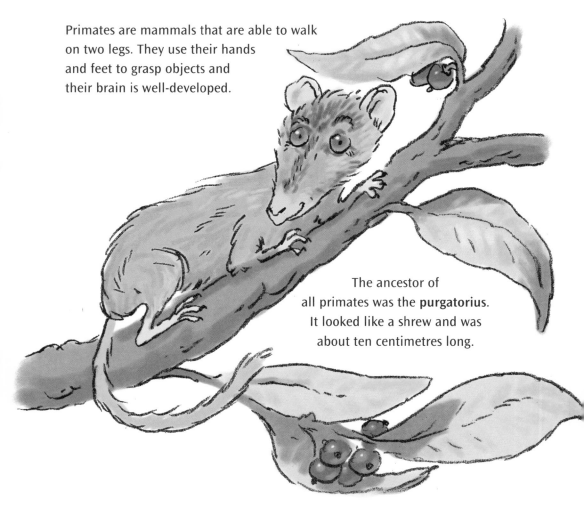

The ancestor of all primates was the **purgatorius**. It looked like a shrew and was about ten centimetres long.

Separation

Around six or seven million years ago, the shared trunk of our family tree divided into two branches: monkeys on one side and the ancestors of modern humans on the other. This separation probably happened because of major shifts in land and climate. The land in Africa split open, creating a barrier between East Africa and the rest of the continent. Our common ancestors living in the west then began to evolve into chimpanzees, and those in the east would become the ancestors of human beings.

The **siamopithecus** was one of the first monkeys, appearing about 40 million years ago. It spent all its time up in the trees. At that time, monkeys like this were developing on almost every continent.

Between man and monkey

In 2009, paleontologists announced they had found a very important skeleton in Ethiopia. It belonged to the oldest human ancestor, a woman they nicknamed Ardi (short for 'Ardipithecus'). Her skeleton is about 4.4 million years old. Ardi would have looked more like a hairy monkey than a human. She had grasping feet (like a chimpanzee) which meant she was good at climbing trees, but she could also walk on two legs, like a human. Her brain was the size of a chimpanzee's, and she would have weighed about 50 kgs.

The next group of early humans were called Australopithecus, named because the first fossils were found in Africa australis, or southern Africa. They appeared around four million years ago, and the last of them died out nearly 1.5 million years ago.

The human family

The history of humankind doesn't run in a straight line. Several different groups existed, some at the same time, from 2.5 million years ago to today.

One and a half million years ago, **Homo habilis** ('handy man') joined the family. These were the first real humans that we know about. Their brains were more developed than their ancestors', and they used stone tools and sticks, a little like chimpanzees and gorillas do today.

Homo ergaster ('craftsman') arrived on the scene between two million and 1.8 million years ago. They were taller than the others, and were fast runners. These were the first humans to leave Africa, and the first to use fire.

Homo erectus ('upright man') appeared in Africa 1.8 million years ago. Tall, strong and resourceful, they became fearsome hunters. Using the sharp-edged tools they made, they were able to attack large animals such as elephants.

Homo neandertalensis ('Neanderthal man') appeared 100,000 years ago. They lived in huts or caves and wore clothing made of animal skins for protection from the cold. They buried their dead.

Homo sapiens ('wise man') appeared about the same time as Neanderthal man. These were the first modern humans. The two species would co-exist for several thousand years, before the Neanderthals died out. This left the way clear for the direct descendants of Homo sapiens – us!

The Homo sapiens originated in Africa and went on to colonise the rest of the world. Physical differences begin to develop from this point, mostly caused by adapting to the climate. People who needed protection from the sun developed darker skin, and those who lived in cold regions were more stockily built.

Homo sapiens were probably the first of our ancestors to use speech. They were also very creative and probably invented art. Cave paintings have been found that date back about 30,000 years.

Why are living creatures different from each other?

Until the 19th century, most scientists and philosophers thought that all living creatures were brought to life instantly, as if by magic. But then a crazy new idea emerged: what if all the different species evolved over billions of years from a single ancestor? The species might seem very different, but when you look closely there are similarities as well.

The evolution revolution

One of the first scientists to believe that living things had changed through the ages was **Buffon**, a French naturalist at the end of the 18th century.

In the mid 19th century, Englishman **Charles Darwin** put forward the most complete theory of evolution. It's still accepted by most scientists today.

At the beginning of the 19th century, French biologist **Jean-Baptiste Lamarck** suggested that plants and animals changed to adapt to their environments. He was on the right track.

Darwin didn't just dream up this theory. It was based on 25 years of observation and research. As a young man he had spent five years sailing round the world studying animals and plants. He became convinced that all species are developed from one another through a series of slow changes, and that their differences are the result of a long process of evolution.

On the Galapagos Islands in the Pacific, Darwin noticed that the beaks of chaffinches varied from one island to the next. He realised that a single species of chaffinch had evolved into several species with different beaks, depending on the kind of food the birds ate on each island.

Natural selection

According to Darwin, no individual is exactly the same as another, even within the same species. The variations between them are the result of chance. It might be a change in the colour of their coat, the disappearance or development of a leg or a wing. In a changing environment, any variations that are a disadvantage mean that, sooner or later, the species will become extinct. On the other hand, if a new variation gives the animal an advantage – making it stronger or faster – it will improve its chances of survival. Darwin called this 'natural selection'. This means that the environment selects what is useful and gets rid of what is not.

These three foxes have variations which depend on where each lives.

The European fox, which lives in the forest, has medium-sized ears.

The Fennec fox, which lives in the hot Saharan desert, has large ears to keep it cool.

The Arctic fox, which lives in cold areas, has tiny rounded ears which won't get frostbite

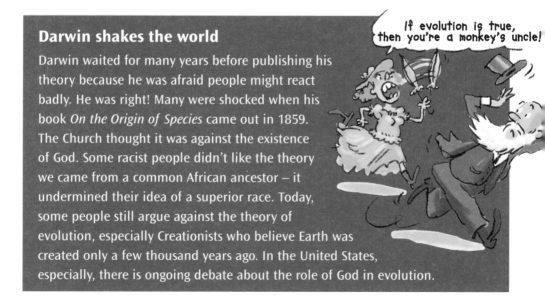

Darwin shakes the world

Darwin waited for many years before publishing his theory because he was afraid people might react badly. He was right! Many were shocked when his book *On the Origin of Species* came out in 1859. The Church thought it was against the existence of God. Some racist people didn't like the theory we came from a common African ancestor – it undermined their idea of a superior race. Today, some people still argue against the theory of evolution, especially Creationists who believe Earth was created only a few thousand years ago. In the United States, especially, there is ongoing debate about the role of God in evolution.

Most of the time, you can't see the changes as a species evolves. There are a few exceptions though, and here is one of the most amazing ones.

In England at the beginning of the 19th century, the **peppered moth** had pale wings. These pale-winged moths blended in with the bark of the silver birch tree, making them safe from predators. By chance, a very small number of them were born with black wings.

Around 1850, pollution from growing industries and factories began to darken the tree trunks. The lighter moths were easily seen and were eaten first; the black ones now had better camouflage, and many more of them survived.

III

LIFE IS A GREAT ADVENTURE

The food chain – eat or be eaten

A caterpillar is busy nibbling on a leaf. Suddenly a sparrow lands and snaps it up. But the bird has barely swallowed when a cat pounces and gobbles it up. This is called a food chain. It links all living creatures together. If any of the links of the chain were to disappear, the whole thing might collapse.

All life forms need energy to stay alive. They draw this energy from other life forms.

Plants take up the nutrients they need from the soil. The plants are eaten by herbivorous animals. Next, the herbivores are eaten by carnivores. These carnivores become the prey of larger carnivores. Finally, micro-organisms and fungi feed on dead bodies and plant remains, which they transform into nutrients that the plants take up from the soil. Everything is linked!

A space for everyone

Many different species share the same territory. How do they manage not to step on each others' toes? Usually, each species has its own way of life. They don't all hunt in the same way, they're not all active at the same time, and they don't all eat the same food …

The **black rhinoceros** eats bushes within its reach.

The **gnu** eats tender new shoots.

Heard the news? The gnus herd!

The **zebra** grazes on long grass.

The giraffe munches on the highest leaves.

The **elephant** pulls leaves and bark off with its trunk.

The gazelle feeds on plants and fruit at ground level.

There is food for all on the African savannah. Each herbivore eats a different plant or part of the plant.

A delicate balance

The survival of a species doesn't just depend on the other creatures it lives with.
It also depends on where it lives – forests, plains, mountains, deserts, lakes, seas.
These environments and the life forms that populate them are called ecosystems.

Each species occupies a particular place (habitat) within its ecosystem, and they're all closely dependent on each other. It's a delicate balance. If there is not enough food for the herbivores, then the carnivores won't have enough meat to survive on.

By hunting certain animals or destroying habitats, humans can cause ecosystems to change. Sometimes a species can become extinct.

Our own little creatures

Billions of tiny creatures are living on and in your body right now! They are so small they're invisible to the naked eye. Most of them are not dangerous and many are actually useful, such as the bacteria in your tummy. They find food in your intestines, and in exchange they help your digestion. Other micro-organisms that live on us, like mites, can cause itching or spread diseases.

A threat to life

Humans are unusual creatures. We are intelligent enough to modify our environment. This began 10,000 years ago, when our ancestors first began to grow food crops and raise animals. But since the 19th century, everything has speeded up. The growth of science and technology has given us the power to impact – and even destroy – the environment on a much larger scale. Many species are under threat.

Around 30% of the planet is covered in forest. But 13 million hectares of forest are disappearing every year – that's like two football fields destroyed every second! The trees are being replaced by roads and crops. Pollution, fires and storms have made things even worse.

Tropical rainforests have been the worst affected. They cover only 7% of the planet, but are home to between 50% and 90% of all plants and animals. Thousands of these tropical species disappear every year.

A single tree in the Amazon jungle can be home to more than 40 different species of ants.

Death by pollution

Chemical fertilisers and pesticides used by farmers trickle down through the soil when it rains. They pollute underground water, which then flows into rivers and springs. Factories release their waste into the rivers, too, and this pollution kills off many species.

Oil spills can create massive ecological disasters. These pools of crude oil floating on the sea may be accidents or could be from ships dumping their oil. Every spill causes the deaths of tens of thousands of animals, and wrecks the coastline.

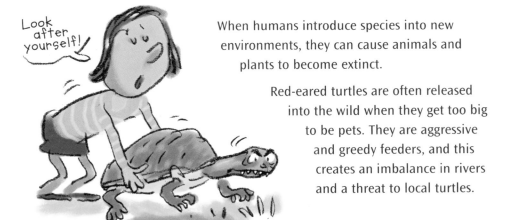

Look after yourself!

When humans introduce species into new environments, they can cause animals and plants to become extinct.

Red-eared turtles are often released into the wild when they get too big to be pets. They are aggressive and greedy feeders, and this creates an imbalance in rivers and a threat to local turtles.

45

Endangered species

Ever since plants and animals have lived on Earth, new species have arrived and others have died out, sometimes from natural disasters, such as the dinosaurs. But the rate of extinction has increased because of human activities. If this keeps up, we will have destroyed half of all plant and animal species by the end of this century.

The **Mediterranean monk seal** is the most endangered species in France, with fewer than 600 seals remaining. Large numbers of tourists on the beaches prevent the seals from giving birth to their young on the sand.

Never buy ivory souvenirs. They are made from **elephants**' tusks. Over the past twenty years, the population of African elephants has dropped from almost one and a half million to only 500,000.

There are five species of rhinoceros in the world, and they are all endangered. There were a million **black rhinos** at the start of the 20th century. Now there are only 4,000 left. Poachers hunt them for their horns, so these are sometimes sawn off to prevent the rhinos being killed.

The **giant panda** has become the symbol of the fight to protect endangered animals. There are only a thousand of these cute bears living on reserves in China. That isn't many, but they are being carefully looked after. Chinese scientists are even trying to clone them.

Gorillas, orang-utans, chimpanzees and bonobos are all **great apes**. They are sometimes hunted for their meat, and can lose their habitat when forests are cut down. They can also be caught in the cross-fire of human wars.

Corals are very useful because they provide a home to nearly two million species of fish, shellfish, worms and crustaceans in the ocean. The rise in sea water temperature and pollution seriously endanger the corals – as do fishing techniques that use dynamite or cyanide.

Protecting the environment

Humans realised a long time ago that we are responsible for most of the plants and animals that have become extinct. It sounds hard to believe, but laws and fines have become necessary to slow down extinctions. Today there are many laws preventing the commercial exploitation of animals and plants.

Since whales were brought to the brink of extinction, the majority of countries no longer hunt them. But Iceland, Japan and Norway are still killing whales, saying it is for scientific research.

Protective organisations

There are many environmental protection organisations fighting pollution and trying to protect endangered species. They sometimes carry out highly-publicised stunts to raise public awareness.

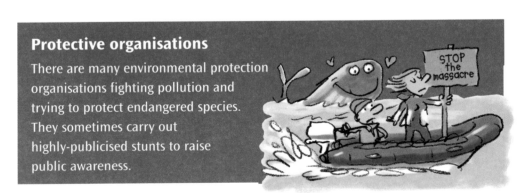

Some areas have been set up as protected zones to help fight the disappearance of life forms. They are chosen because of the range and richness of species living there. They are usually called national parks or reserves. Humans can no longer do whatever they like in these areas and, in some cases, only scientists have the right to go there.

Of course, it's impossible to put a protective cover over the entire planet. So wherever possible, humans should try to live in harmony with nature.

For example, we can bury high voltage power lines in the ground so that birds are not electrocuted, or we can build tunnels so that frogs can cross roads safely to breed in their favourite pond.

You can follow these simple rules:

Don't pick protected plants.

Don't disturb birds and animals, especially during the breeding season.

Set up a nesting-box for birds, or let part of your garden grow wild to encourage bees and insects.

Giving life

From the tiniest bacteria to the largest whales, all living creatures are capable of giving birth. That's how life spreads across our planet.

There are two kinds of reproduction. Some organisms (such as bacteria and worms) can reproduce on their own – by cutting themselves in two, for example. This is 'asexual reproduction', and the offspring is identical to its parent.

Most animals and plants have 'sexual reproduction', meaning that a male and a female must unite. This makes for very varied offspring.

Fertilisation

In animals, the female and the male each have different sex cells. The female has a round ovum, or egg. The male has sperm that look like little tadpoles. For a new life to be created, an ovum and a sperm have to come into contact with each other. This is called fertilisation.

For many animals, fertilisation takes place inside the female's body after the male puts his penis into the female's vagina. With mammals, including humans, the egg develops inside the mother's womb.

Settle down, kiddies!

With fish and frogs, fertilisation takes place outside their bodies. The female releases her ova into the water and the male covers them with his sperm. The fertilised ova develop into eggs, then into tadpoles or baby fish.

In flowering plants, the male cells are found in pollen which is produced by the stamens. Female cells are in the pistil. By carrying the pollen from one flower to another, wind and insects make sure fertilisation takes place.

Multiplying cells

As soon as fertilisation has occurred, the egg divides into two new cells. Each of these then divides in two again, to make four, then eight, then sixteen cells, and so on, until all these cells make a complete living creature.

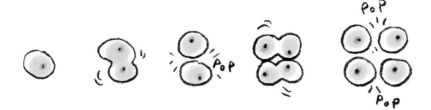

Inside the mother's womb

The gestation period is not the same for every animal. A mother elephant has to wait for 22 months until she gives birth, but a mouse keeps the babies in her womb for just 20 days.

Birth

Birds lay their eggs in a nest. They sit on them to warm them with their bodies. The chicks have to make a big effort to break out of the shell.

When kittens are born, their mother cuts through the umbilical cord with her teeth. Then she licks the babies to remove the membrane that covered them inside her uterus.

Lizards and snakes lay their eggs on the ground or under fallen leaves, but they don't sit on them. The eggs are warmed by the soil and the sun. The babies have to hatch by themselves. They break the egg by using a little tooth on the end of their snout.

Many mammals lie down to give birth, but the giraffe stays on her feet. The baby giraffe pushes itself out, and then it falls two metres to the ground. That's quite a drop for a baby!

Nine months until birth

A human baby stays safely inside its mother's womb for about nine months.

At 1 month

The developing baby is called an embryo. It's the size of a
pea and already has a beating heart.

At 2 months

It is three centimetres long, with
arms and legs, hands and feet.

At 3 months

The embryo is no more than ten
centimetres long, but the organs inside its body are
already formed. From this point on it's called a foetus.

At 4 months

The foetus is 15 centimetres long. It has nails and hair. It can sit up, turn around,
stretch and kick. Its mother can feel it moving.

Amniotic liquid
surrounds the baby.

The **umbilical cord**
links the baby
to the placenta.

The **uterus**
expands as
the baby grows.

The **placenta** provides
it with oxygen and
nourishment.

At 5 months

The foetus can hear its mother's tummy
rumbling, and some outside noises like
laughter, music, shouting and car horns.

At 6 months

The baby is 30 centimetres long.
It swallows amniotic liquid and pees into it,
but the liquid is automatically cleaned.

At 7 months

The baby sleeps nearly all the time.
It's starting to feel a bit cramped.

At 8 months

The baby turns around in the uterus to get ready for birth: the head points downwards, the hips at the top.

At 9 months

It's a tight fit for the baby now. At about 50 centimetres long, it weighs a little over three kilograms. It is time for it to leave the cosy nest. The mother's muscles contract to push the baby downwards. Her vagina opens to let the baby pass through, head first.

Once out, it cries for the first time – a good sign! The midwife cuts the umbilical cord and hands the newborn baby to the mother. It is a very emotional moment for the parents.

Heredity

You've probably heard people say, 'He's got his father's pointy nose', or 'She's got her mother's curly hair'. You look like your parents because they have each passed on to you a part of themselves. This is called heredity. Every cell of your body contains coded information called genes. These genes are responsible for the colour of your hair and eyes, and the shape of your face.

Learning to grow

Everything that lives, grows. Some species take a few days to reach full size, and others take several years. Human and animal babies have to eat a great deal to grow bigger and heavier.

Baby mice are born hairless and blind. At 14 days, they have all their fur. At three weeks, they begin to leave the nest. From two or three months old, they are fully grown and able to have their own babies.

3 days   3 weeks   3 months

At birth, **bear cubs** weigh 300 grams. They reach three kilograms in two months thanks to the goodness of their mother's milk. At six months, they are already eating an adult diet but still stay close to their mother. Male bears keep growing until they are ten years old, but females reach their final size by the time they are five.

6 days   6 months   6 years

Human beings grow very quickly to begin with. In its first year, a baby grows more than 20 centimetres and triples its birth weight. By the age of four it has doubled in height to be about one metre tall. After that it grows at least four millimetres every month until the age of 13. During adolescence, growth speeds up again. Around the age of 20 it reaches a final height as the bones stop growing.

I might be the smallest, but I'm growing the fastest!

| 1 month | 4 years | 13 years | 20 years |

Growing and learning

During the early years, babies concentrate on growing. After this they begin to learn to control their movements, to walk, talk and read. They discover how to use their hands, how to dress themselves, to learn right from left, and how to make friends.

Healthy eating for healthy living

No living creature can survive without
eating and drinking. Inside your
body, food is transformed into the
energy you need to grow and stay
healthy. That's why it's important
to eat a balanced diet – you should
eat a little of everything.

Oil, butter and cream contain
fats. They give your body lots of
energy, but you need only
small amounts of them.

Bread, cereals, rice and pasta contain sugars,
called **carbohydrates**. They release energy
to the body over several hours.

Fruit and vegetables are
rich in **vitamins** which play
an important role in your
body. For example, vitamin
A is needed for growth and
for the skin; vitamin C
helps to fight against
diseases.

Milk, yoghurt and cheese contain **calcium** which makes your bones and teeth strong. Growing children need a lot of it.

Meat, fish and eggs contain **proteins**. These are the essential building blocks of cells. Proteins are vital for growth and help keep you healthy.

We need to drink about one and a half litres of **water** every day.

Staying healthy

Being healthy means being able to fight off diseases easily. You need to exercise regularly to make your body strong, and keep it clean so that microbes can't multiply. There's nothing better than a good night's sleep to make you full of energy. A child of ten needs to sleep about ten hours a day. You should also see a doctor occasionally to check that everything is working properly and get vaccinated against serious diseases.

Puberty

When girls are between the ages of nine and 13, and boys are between 11 and 15, the body changes and begins to look more and more like a grown-up's. This is called puberty.

Boys start to grow hair all over their bodies. Their voices change and get deeper.

Girls' breasts will develop. Hair starts to grow under their arms and between their legs.

The biggest changes are hidden. The sexual organs start to function at puberty. A boy's penis grows larger and his testicles produce sperm. A girl's ovaries release ova. Every month, the membrane inside her uterus swells with blood, ready to start growing a baby. If fertilisation doesn't happen, the blood is released. This is called menstruation or 'having a period'. When a girl gets her period, it means her body is physically able to have a baby.

Your body isn't the only thing that changes during puberty. There are challenging things going on in your head too. You want to have more freedom and wear whatever you want. Boys are interested in girls and girls start to be interested in boys. Your parents may annoy you, and you may spend hours with your friends. You're not always easy to get along with! It takes time to feel comfortable with the new you.

Every story must end

All living creatures will die one day. That's the way life is. Ageing is programmed into every one of our cells. Over the years, humans and animals become less supple and get tired faster. Their eyesight gets worse, they don't hear as well, and their bodies have trouble fighting diseases. One day, the heart stops beating.

How long do animals live?

It is hard to know how long wild animals will live. They probably live longer in zoos where they are cared for and protected. In the wild, a slow, elderly animal would be soon eaten!

Tortoise: 100 years.

Dog: 20 years.

Elephant: 80 years.

Rabbit: 15 years.

Ant: 2 years.

Horse: 50 years.

Chimpanzee: 50 years.

Queen bee: 5 years.

Mouse: 3 years.

Cat: 20 years.

Dolphin: 30 years.

Mayfly: 1 or 2 days.

Hey, that's not fair!

When an animal or plant dies, it doesn't go to waste. Vultures, insects and worms feast on the body. Anything left over goes back into the soil to nourish the plants.

Hare today, gone tomorrow!

According to the statistics, I've got 68 years left and you've got 64 ...

But what's the margin of error?

Humans

Humans are living longer and longer thanks to medical advances and improved living conditions. In the UK, Australia and New Zealand, women live to 82 years on average, and men to an average age of 78 years. In very poor countries, living conditions are more difficult. There, the average life span is only about 50 years and many children die from lack of proper care, and malnutrition.

Cloning

In 1996, a team of Scottish scientists succeeded in producing the first clone of an adult mammal – a sheep named Dolly. Unlike other ewes, Dolly had no father and was conceived from her mother alone, a bit like a photocopy. Some people thought this was a major scientific advance and there have been many cloning experiments since. Sometimes the goal is therapeutic cloning which, rather than cloning an individual, aims to produce replacement cells for the treatment of diseases. Some people believe they will be able to save endangered species this way.

Don't copy me!

Don't copy me!

Many people are concerned about experiments with human cloning. It's possible this could lead to 'designer' babies: parents could choose a particular height, hair, eye, and skin colour. In some countries (such as France) the law forbids reproductive and therapeutic human cloning. In other countries (including England), experiments on human embryos are allowed.

As people age, their bodies get weaker, their memories may fail, or they may become dependent on others. Some are not able to shop or prepare meals for themselves, so they can no longer live alone. But people's brains can remain active well into old age, especially if they try to always learn new things.

An organism needs oxygen to live. When the heart stops, the blood stops circulating and oxygen no longer reaches the cells. This causes the brain to stop functioning, and a person is said to be brain dead. At that point life has ended.

Death makes life possible

It would be a catastrophe if no human, animal or plant ever died – it would be very crowded! The planet's natural balance would be threatened. Death allows evolution to happen, thanks to the appearance of new characteristics from one generation to the next. Although all lives come to an end, each one is different, and each has something to offer the world. That's what makes life so fascinating.

It's not easy to imagine things that last for millions or billions of years. So let's 'shrink' the history of Earth to one year, starting on 1 January.

This would mean that life first appeared in the first week of March. The first vertebrates emerged from the water on 20 November. The dinosaurs disappeared on 26 December. The first modern humans were born in the night of 28 December. Captain James Cook first visited New Zealand only one and a half seconds ago!

If Earth was one year old

67

Life quiz

Now that you're an expert on the beginning of the world and the evolution of living creatures, have some fun asking adults these questions.

1. How many known species are there on Earth?

2. What is the name of Darwin's revolutionary theory?

3. Homo erectus was the first human to make cave paintings.

☐ True ☐ False

4. Every living creature needs two main things. What are they?

5. What do we call the event that brought the universe into being?

6. The first life forms came into existence on the land.

☐ True ☐ False

7. What do we call the tiny structures that every life form is made up of?

8. What amphibian lives on the banks of pools and ponds?

69

9. The word dinosaur means 'devil lizard'.

☐ True ☐ False

10. What do we call the remains of a plant or animal that has become part of the rock?

11. Are humans responsible for the disappearance of the dinosaurs?

12. What do we call a person who studies prehistoric plants and animals?

13. Darwin's idea called 'natural selection' means that the environment selects what is useless. True or false?

14. What is the word used to describe the passing on of certain characteristics from a person to his or her children?

15. The first cloned animal was a hooflung.

☐ True ☐ False

16. Humans and monkeys share a common ancestor.

☐ True ☐ False

17. How many people are there on Earth?

18. Australian forests are the most damaged by deforestation.

☐ True ☐ False

ANSWERS

I've finished marking your tests ...

1. 1.7 million

2. The theory of evolution.

3. False. It was Homo sapiens.

4. Air and water.

5. The Big Bang.

6. False. They were born in the water.

7. Cells.

8. Frog.

9. False. It means terrible lizard.

10. A fossil.

11. No. Dinosaurs were probably victims of a meteorite impact, and there were no humans living at that time.

12. A paleontologist.

13. False.

14. Heredity.

15. False. It was a sheep called Dolly.

16. True. It's a small primate.

17. Nearly seven billion.

18. False. Tropical rainforests are the worst affected.

Mini dictionary

Amphibian
An animal that is able to live in the air or the water.

Atmosphere
The layers of gases that surround Earth and protect it from the Sun's rays.

Bacteria
Tiny life forms made of a single cell.

Big Bang
According to Big Bang theory, the universe was formed following a gigantic explosion 13.7 billion years ago.

Cell
The basic structural unit of a life form. Plants, animals and humans are made up of billions of tiny cells.

Clone
An organism that is genetically identical to another organism, created without the union of male and female.

DNA
Molecule containing the genes, in the cell nucleus.

Ecosystem
A natural environment and the life forms that inhabit it.

Embryo
The name given to the developing baby during the first three months in the mother's womb.

Erosion
Damage done to terrain over time by wind, water, frost ...

Fossil
Prints or remains of animals or plants found in rock.

Galaxy
An immense grouping of stars.

Gene
Part of the nucleus of a cell that transmits hereditary characteristics (like eye colour).

Gestation
Period during which the female carries her young before they are born.

Invertebrates
Creatures without any bones inside their bodies.

Mammal
A vertebrate animal, generally having body hair. The female has mammary glands to suckle her young.

Naturalist
Scientist who studies plants, minerals and animals.

Ovaries
Glands of women and female mammals which produce ova.

Ovum (plural ova)
Female sex cell of a living creature; egg.

Ozone layer
Layer of the upper atmosphere made up of a gas called ozone. The ozone layer filters out the Sun's dangerous rays.

Paleontologist
Scientist who studies prehistoric animals and plants.

Pesticide
Chemical that kills animal and plant pests (but it can also poison non-pest creatures).

Pistil
Female sex organ of flowers.

Pollen
Yellow powder produced by the stamens of flowers, and used in fertilisation.

Puberty
The physical and psychological changes that happen between childhood to adulthood.

Reserve
An area set aside and controlled to protect all or some of the plant and animal species living within it.

Sediment
Deposit left by water or wind.

Species
A grouping of living creatures that look similar and can breed to produce fertile offspring.

Sperm
Male reproductive cell.

Stamen
Male sex organ of a flower, where pollen is formed.

Testicles
The sexual glands of men and male animals that produce sperm.

Uterus
In women and female mammals, the organ inside which the embryo develops. Also called the womb.

Vertebrates
Creatures with skeletons inside their bodies.

Some useful websites

www.sdnhm.org/kids/dinosaur

www.esa.int/esaKIDSen/OurUniverse.html

www.biology4kids.com